Windows to the Sky

Live not without a God! however low or high,
In every house should be a window to the sky.
W. W. Story

Windows to the Sky

Compiled by Caesar Johnson

Designed and illustrated by Gordon Brown

Published by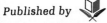

The C. R. Gibson Company

Norwalk, Connecticut

Windows to

Complete acknowledgments
appear at the back of the book.

The world in which we live is a world of human beings who do the good, the bad, the useless, the noble, the brave, the foolish and the wise things. No man exists alone, for everyone of us is touched by other people.

We may begin our lives by giving love to one other human being, but if we are wise, that love extends to family, friends, our little world and so to all humanity. Each one of us sees life through his own window. In this book are views of life as other people see it.

Windows to Love

Love means the body, the soul,
the life, the entire being.
We feel love as we feel the warmth
of our blood, we breathe love
as we breathe air, we hold it in
ourselves as we hold our thoughts.
Nothing more exists for us.

Guy De Maupassant

To love is to place our happiness
in the happiness of another.

Gottfried von Leibnitz

It is a beautiful necessity of our nature
to love something.

Douglas Jerrold

Love is two souls with but a single thought,
Two hearts that beat as one.

Von Münch Bellinghausen

Love is a strange bewilderment which overtakes
one person on account of another person.

James Thurber and E. B. White

Give all to love,
Obey thy heart.

Ralph Waldo Emerson

Heart of my heart, the world is young;
Love lies hidden in every rose.

Alfred Noyes

There is nothing holier in this life of ours
than the first consciousness of love.

Henry Wadsworth Longfellow

With thee all tales are sweet; each clime
has charms; earth — sea alike — our world
within our arms.

Lord Byron

Love does not consist in gazing at each
other but in looking outward together
in the same direction.

Antoine de Saint-Exupéry

There's nothing half so sweet in life
As love's young dream.

Thomas Moore

Love is a pleasing but various clime.

William Shenstone

Take love away from life and you take
away its pleasure.

Jean Baptiste Molière

When you fish for love, bait with your
heart, not your brain.

Mark Twain

Love gives itself; it is not bought.

Henry Wadsworth Longfellow

Love is a canvas furnished by Nature
and embroidered by imagination.

Voltaire

May was never the month of love,
For May is full of flowers;
But rather April, wet by kind,
For love is full of showers.

Robert Southwell

True love is always young in the heart.

Honoré de Balzac

If a woman doesn't chase a man a little,
she doesn't love him.

E. W. Howe

The quarrels of lovers are the renewal of love.

Terrence

We love being in lovè, that's the truth on't.

William Makepeace Thackeray

We are shaped and fashioned by what we love.

Johann Wolfgang von Goethe

Life is a flower of which love is the honey.

Victor Hugo

Love is a madness most discreet.

William Shakespeare

Oh, love, love, love!
Love is like a dizziness,
It winna let a poor body
Go about his biziness.

James Hogg

O Love, O fire! once he drew
With one long kiss my whole soul thro'
My lips, as sunlight drinketh dew.

Alfred, Lord Tennyson

Love is never lost. If not reciprocated it will
flow back and soften and purify the heart.

Washington Irving

Ah! what is love? It is a pretty thing,
As sweet unto a shepherd as a king.

Robert Greene

To love is to be all made of sighs and tears.

William Shakespeare

And I, what is my crime I cannot tell,
Unless it be a crime t' have lov'd too well.

Richard Crashaw

The silver link, the silken tie,
Which heart to heart, and mind to mind,
In body and in soul can bind.

Sir Walter Scott

Tell me, dearest, what is love?
'Tis a lightning from above;
'Tis an arrow, 'tis a fire,
'Tis a boy they call desire.

Beaumont and Fletcher

If you would be loved, love and be lovable.

Benjamin Franklin

There is no remedy for love but to love more.

Henry Thoreau

Many waters cannot quench love,
neither can the floods drown it.

Song of Solomon

There is no living in love without suffering.

Thomas à Kempis

Pain of love be sweeter far
Than all other pleasures are.

John Dryden

All who joy would win must share it.
Happiness was born a twin.

Lord Byron

Nor steel nor fire itself hath power
Like woman in her conquering hour.
Be thou but fair, mankind adore thee,
Smile, and a world is weak before thee.

Thomas Moore

They love least that let men know their love.

William Shakespeare

The word 'imposition' is never used
where there is love.

Albert Einstein

Man, in carving his future, usually finds
a woman the mallet behind his chisel.

Arthur Stringer

All's fair in love and war.

Francis Smedley

Love, then hath every bliss in store;
'Tis friendship and 'tis something more.
Each other every wish they give;
Not to know love is not to live.

John Gay

A supreme love is a motive that gives
a sublime rhythm to a woman's life.

George Eliot

Love is a second life; it grows into the soul,
warms every vein, and beats in every pulse.

Joseph Addison

We learn only from those we love.

Johann Wolfgang von Goethe

Love is an appetite of generation
by the mediation of beauty.

Socrates

At the touch of love everyone becomes a poet.

Plato

That is the true season of love, when we believe
that we alone can love, that no one
could ever have loved so before us, and
that no one will love in the same way as us.

Johann Wolfgang von Goethe

Love is a circle, that doth restless move
In the same sweet eternity of love.

Robert Herrick

What is Love? I have met in the streets
a very poor young man who was in love.
His hat was old, his coat worn, the water
passed through his shoes and the stars
through his soul.

Victor Hugo

When the one man loves the one woman and
the one woman loves the one man, the very
angels desert heaven and come and sit in
that house and sing for joy.

Brahman — Sutra

Love is the poetry of the senses.

Honoré de Balzac

True love is eternal, infinite,
and always like itself.

Honoré de Balzac

It is better to have loved and lost
Than never to have loved at all.

Alfred, Lord Tennyson

Love is known to be a lovely and a fearful thing.

Lord Byron

15

To love is to believe, to hope, to know:
'Tis an essay, a taste of heaven below!

Edmund Waller

The treasures of the deep are not so
precious as are the concealed comforts
of a man locked up in a woman's love.

Thomas Middleton

Love is a green isle in the sea,
a fountain and a shrine.

Edgar Allen Poe

Talk not of wasted affection, affection
   never was wasted:
If it enrich not the heart of another,
   it's waters returning
Back to the spring, like the rain, shall
   fill them full of refreshment;
That which the fountain sends forth returns
   again to the fountain.

Henry Wadsworth Longfellow

Love is an endeavor to form a friendship
inspired by beauty.

Cicero

Love is not love which does not sweeter live
For having something dreadful to forgive.

Coventry Patmore

When the last night's solemn shadows
Settle dark on you and me,
May the love that never faileth
Take our souls eternally.

J. G. Holland

True love's the gift that God has given
To man alone beneath the heaven.

Sir Walter Scott

Love looks through a telescope, envy
through a microscope.

George Bernard Shaw

Love is the noblest frailty of the mind.

John Dryden

Our work shall still be better for our love,
And still our love be sweeter for our work.

Elizabeth Barrett Browning

We are all born for love: it is the
principle of existence and its only end.

Benjamin Disraeli

In dreams and love there are no impossibilities.

János Arany

Love sought is good, but given unsought is better.

William Shakespeare

Love is swift, sincere, pious, pleasant,
gentle, strong, patient, faithful, prudent,
long-suffering, manly, and never seeking her own.

Thomas à Kempis

Love comforteth like sunshine after rain.

William Shakespeare

When there is love in the heart, there
are rainbows in the eyes, which cover
every black cloud with gorgeous hues.

Henry Ward Beecher

He is not a lover who does not love forever.

Euripides

Art and religion are the soul of civilization.
Go to them, for there love exists.

Frank Lloyd Wright

Life is ever Lord of death,
And love can never lose its own.

John Greenleaf Whittier

Mutual love, the crown of all our bliss.

John Milton

The light of a whole life dies when love is done.

F. W. Bourdillon

To live without love is not really to live.

Jean Baptiste Molière

It is the very essence of love,
of nobleness, of greatness, to be willing
to suffer for the good of others.

Herbert Spencer

True love is the ripe fruit of a lifetime.

Lamartine

Love is the crowning grace of humanity,
the holiest right of the soul.

Francesco Petrarch

Love is an image of God, and not a lifeless
image, but the living essence of the divine
nature which beams full of goodness.

Martin Luther

To love is to know the sacrifices which
eternity exacts from man.

John Hobbes

Two human loves make one divine.

Elizabeth Barrett Browning

Love is the emblem of eternity: it confounds
all notion of time: effaces all memory
of a beginning, all fear of an end.

Madame de Staël

The purest joy we can experience in one
we love is to see that person a source of
happiness to others.

Unknown

O, my luv is like a red, red rose
That's newly sprung in June . . .
O, my luv is like a melodie
That's sweetly play'd in tune.

Robert Burns

Windows to Marriage

A happy marriage has
in it all the pleasures
of friendship, all the
enjoyments of sense and
reason, and, indeed,
all the sweets of life.

Joseph Addison

A successful marriage is an edifice
that must be rebuilt every day.

André Maurois

The happiness of married life depends upon making
small sacrifices with readiness and cheerfulness.

John Seldon

Ay, marriage is the life-long miracle,
The self-begetting wonder, daily fresh.

Charles Kingsley

The one word above all others that makes
marriage successful is 'ours.'

Robert Quillen

There is more of good nature than of
good sense at the bottom of most marriages.

Henry Thoreau

The highest happiness on earth is in marriage.
Every man who is happily married is a successful
man even if he has failed in everything else.

William Lyon Phelps

It is not marriage that fails; it is the
people that fail. All that marriage does
is show people up.

Harry Emerson Fosdick

Marriage enlarges the scene of our
happiness and of our miseries.

Joseph Addison

In married conversation, as in surgery,
the knife must be used with care.

André Maurois

Rising early and marrying young
are what no man ever repents of.

Martin Luther

Marriage! Nothing else demands so much from a man!

Henrik Ibsen

Hasty marriage seldom proveth well.

William Shakespeare

They dream in courtship, but in wedlock wake.

Alexander Pope

Keep your eyes wide open before marriage
and half-shut afterwards.

Benjamin Franklin

Let me not to the marriage of true minds
Admit impediments.

William Shakespeare

I do not, however, pretend to have discovered
that life has anything more to be desired
than a prudent and virtuous marriage.

Samuel Johnson

Where there is marriage without love,
there will be love without marriage.

Benjamin Franklin

A good marriage rejects the company and
conditions of love. It endeavors to present
those of friendship.

Michel de Montaigne

The wife is the key of the house.

Thomas Fuller

Start saying nice things to your wife,
even if it terrifies her at first.

Unknown

Marriage with a good woman is a harbour
in the tempest of life; with a bad woman,
it is a tempest in the harbour.

J. P. Senn

Woman, dear woman, still the same
While beauty breathes through soul or frame:
While man possesses heart and eyes,
Woman's bright empire never dies.

Thomas Moore

Grave authors say, and witty poets sing,
That honest wedlock is a glorious thing.

Alexander Pope

I believe it will be found that those who marry late
are best pleased with their children, and those
who marry early, with their partners.

Samuel Johnson

Marriage must be a relation either of
sympathy or of conquest.

George Eliot

Marriage is not commonly unhappy,
otherwise than as life is unhappy.

Samuel Johnson

A wife's pleasures are in the happiness of her family.

Jean Jacques Rousseau

Men have marble, women waxen, minds.

William Shakespeare

When men enter into the state of marriage,
they stand nearest to God.

Henry Ward Beecher

Women have a less accurate measure of time
than men. There is a clock in Adam: none in Eve.

Ralph Waldo Emerson

Women are wiser than men because they
know less and understand more.

James Stephens

Some respite to husbands the weather may send,
But housewives' affairs have never an end.

Thomas Tusser

Man wants but little here below,
He is not hard to please;
But woman — bless her little heart!
Wants everything she sees.

Park Benjamin

The happy married man dies in good stile at home,
surrounded by his weeping wife and children.
The old bachelor don't die at all—
he sort of rots away, like a pollywog's tail.

Artemus Ward

One should believe in marriage as in the
immortality of the soul.

Honoré de Balzac

Marriage, rightly understood
Gives to the tender and the good
A paradise below.

John Cotton

If for accomplishments — more of the spirit
Than beauty, or riches, or honors — you'd strive,
Endeavor a sensible woman to merit,
For charms of the soul must all others survive.

Samuelson

Nobody works so hard for his money
as the man who marries it.

Elbert Hubbard

From my experience, not one in twenty
marries the first love; we build statues
of snow and weep to see them melt.

Sir Walter Scott

If you would have the nuptial union last,
Let virtue be the bond that ties it fast.

Nicholas Rowe

The perfect woman is as beautiful as she
is strong, as tender as she is sensible.
She is calm, deliberate, dignified, leisurely.
She is gay, graceful, sprightly,
sympathetic. She is severe upon occasion,
and upon occasion playful. She has fancies,
dreams, romances, ideas. She organizes
neatness, and order, and comfort, but they
are merely the foundation wherein rises
the temple of her home, beautiful for
situation, the joy of the whole earth.

Gail Hamilton

Love in marriage should be the
accomplishment of a beautiful dream,
and not, as it often is, the end.

Alphonse Karr

No happiness is like unto it, no love so
great as that of man and wife, no such
comfort as a sweet wife.

Robert Burton

My wife is one of the best wimin on the
continent, altho' she isn't always gentle
as a lamb, with mint sauce.

Artemus Ward

A man is in general better pleased when
he has had a good dinner upon his table,
than when his wife talks Greek.

Samuel Johnson

Next to no wife, a good wife is best.

Thomas Fuller

Being a husband is a whole-time job.
That is why so many husbands fail.

Arnold Bennett

The calmest husbands make the stormiest wives.

Thomas Dekker

Love is the magician, the enchanter,
that changes worthless things to joy.

Robert Ingersoll

It is not lack of love but lack of friendship
that makes unhappy marriages.

Fredrich Nietzsche

Every man who is high up loves to think
he has done it himself; and the wife
smiles, and lets it go at that.

J. M. Barrie

How much the wife is dearer than the bride.

Lord George Lyttleton

To take a wife merely as an agreeable and
rational companion will commonly be found
to be a grand mistake.

Lord Chesterfield

All other goods by fortune's hand are given,
A wife is the peculiar gift of heaven.

Alexander Pope

The kindest and the happiest pair
Will find occasion to forbear;
And something, every day they live,
To pity, and perhaps forgive.

William Cowper

A happy marriage is a long conversation
that always seems too short.

André Maurois

The sanctity of marriage and the family
relation make the corner-stone of our
American society and civilization.

James Garfield

The first bond of society is marriage;
then children; then the family.

Cicero

I regard marriage as the holiest institution
among men. Without the fireside there is
no human advancement; without the family
relation there is no life worth living.

Robert Ingersoll

What is there in the vale of life
Half so delightful as a wife,
When friendship, love, and peace combine
To stamp the marriage-bond divine?

William Cowper

The highest gift and favor of God is a
pious, kind, godly, and domestic wife,
with whom thou mayest live peaceably,
and to whom thou mayest intrust all thy
possessions, yea thy body and thy life.

Martin Luther

Windows to Family

God looks down well pleased to mark
In earth's dusk each rosy spark,
Lights of home and lights of love,
And the child the heart thereof.

Katharine Hinkson

Family life is the most precious thing in the world.

Charles Eliot

Home's not merely four square walls,
Though with pictures hung and gilded;
Home is where Affection calls,—
Filled with shrines the heart hath builded.

Charles Swain

All happy families resemble each other,
each unhappy family is unhappy in its own way.

Leo Tolstoy

We receive love — from our children as well
as others — not in proportion to our demands
or sacrifices or needs, but roughly
in proportion to our own capacity to love.

Rollo May

What was wonderful about childhood is
that anything in it was a wonder. It
was not merely a world of miracles;
it was a miraculous world.

G. K. Chesterton

A home is the total contribution of love on
the part of each one dwelling within it.

Anne Pannell

A child is a pledge of immortality.

John Newman

Joy dwells beneath a humble roof;
Heaven is not built of country seats
But little queer suburban streets.

Christopher Morley

Our early days! How often back
We turn, on life's bewildering track,
To where, o'er hill and valley, plays
The sunlight of our early days.

Nicholas Rowe

Of all nature's gifts to the human race, what
is more pleasant to a man than his children?

Cicero

Next to God we are indebted to woman,
first for life itself, and then
for making it worth living.

C. N. Bovee

Certain it is that there is no kind of
affection so purely angelic as the love
of a father to a daughter.

Joseph Addison

A woman should be as proud of her success
in making her house into a perfect little
world as the greatest statesman of his
organizing a nation's affairs.

André Maurois

The greatest poem ever known
Is one all poets have outgrown:
The poetry, innate, untold,
Of being only four years old.

Christopher Morley

A boy's will is the wind's will,
And the thoughts of youth are long,
    long thoughts.

Henry Wadsworth Longfellow

How many a father have I seen,
A sober man, among his boys,
Whose youth was full of foolish noise.

Alfred, Lord Tennyson

You can no more measure a home by inches,
or weigh it by ounces, than you can set
up boundaries of a summer breeze, or
calculate the fragrance of a rose. Home is
the love which is in it.

Edward Whiting

You are a King by your own Fireside, as
much as any Monarch on his Throne.

Miguel de Cervantes

Where children are not, heaven is not.

A. C. Swinburne

Sweet is the smile of home; the mutual look,
When hearts are of each other sure.

John Keble

Never did I meet with a father that would
not cheerfully part with his last shilling
to save or bless his son.

N. K. Daggett

One father is more than a hundred schoolmasters.

George Herbert

You don't raise heroes, you raise sons.
And if you treat them like sons, they'll
turn out to be heroes, even if it's just
in your own eyes.

Walter Schirra

The most important thing a father can do
for his children is to love their mother.

Unknown

In all this cold and hollow world, no fount
Of deep, strong, deathless love, save that within
A mother's heart.

Felicia Hemans

Behold the child, by nature's kindly law
Pleased with a rattle, tickled with a straw.

Alexander Pope

Heaven lies about us in our infancy.

William Wordsworth

Men are what their mothers made them.

Ralph Waldo Emerson

When children stand still,
They have done some ill.

A. B. Cheales

The burnt child shuns the fire, until the next day.

Mark Twain

Of all people children are the most imaginative.

Thomas Babington Macauley

I do not remember a single instance of a
young fellow going to the bad who was
tenderly devoted to his parents.

Thain Davidson

Mother is the name for God in the lips
and hearts of little children.

William Makepeace Thackeray

A mother who is really a mother is never free.

Honoré de Balzac

Eat no green apples or you'll droop,
Be careful not to get the croup,
Avoid the chicken-pox and such,
And don't fall out of windows much.

Edward Anthony

A mother is not a person to lean on, but
a person to make leaning unnecessary.

Dorothy Canfield Fisher

Childhood whose very happiness is love.

Letitia Landon

A child is a curly, dimpled lunatic.

Ralph Waldo Emerson

How beautiful is youth! how bright it gleams
With its illusions, aspirations, dreams!
Book of beginnings, story without end,
Each maid a heroine, and each man a friend!

Henry Wadsworth Longfellow

It is very nice to think
The world is full of meat and drink,
With little children saying grace
In every Christian kind of place.

Robert Louis Stevenson

Little children are still the symbol of the
eternal marriage between love and duty.

George Eliot

It is a wise father who knows his own son.

William Shakespeare

Young men are apt to think themselves
wise enough, as drunken men are to think
themselves sober enough.

Lord Chesterfield

The denunciation of the young is a necessary
part of the hygiene of elderly people, and
greatly assists the circulation of the blood.

Logan Pearsall Smith

What greater ornament to a son than a father's glory,
or to a father than a son's honorable conduct.

Sophocles

The future destiny of a child
is always the work of the mother.

Napoleon Bonaparte

Boys and girls tumbling in the street,
and playing, are moving jewels.

Thomas Traherne

Home, — the nursery of the infinite.

W. E. Channing

The hills are dearest which our childish
feet have climbed earliest.

James Greenleaf Whittier

If you want to see what children can do,
stop giving them things.

Norman Douglas

Parents scarcely bring up children now;
they finance them.

John Brooks

Oh! through the world, where'er we roam,
Though souls be pure, and lips be kind,
The heart with fondness turns to home,
Still turns to those it left behind.

Thomas Moore

He who gives a child a treat
Makes joy-bells ring in Heaven's street,
And he who gives a child a home
Builds palaces in Kingdom come.

John Masefield

I like 'em all, babies and all. Boys are
a great care, but darn it, they're worth it.

William Sumner

Money won't buy peace in the home, but
sometimes it will negotiate an armistice.

Raymond Duncan

Woman knows what man has long forgotten,
that the ultimate economic and spiritual
unit of any civilization is still the family.

Clare Boothe Luce

Anyone can build a house; we need the
Lord for the creation of a home.

Benjamin Jowett

Domestic Happiness, thou only bliss of
Paradise that has survived the Fall!

William Cowper

Where there is room in the heart there is
always room in the house.

Thomas Moore

Abstracted from home, I know no happiness
in this world.

> Thomas Jefferson

A comfortable house is a great source of
happiness. It ranks immediately after
health and a good conscience.

> Sydney Smith

Train up a child in the way he should go —
and walk there yourself once in awhile.

> Josh Billings

One laugh of a child will make the
holiest day more sacred still.

> Robert Ingersoll

Love your children with all your hearts,
love them enough to discipline them before
it is too late.

> Lavina Fugal

The strength of a nation, especially
a republican nation, is in the intelligent
and well-ordered homes of the people.

> Mrs. Sigourney

Lo, children are the heritage of the Lord:
and the fruit of the womb is his reward.
As arrows are in the hand of a mighty man;
so are children of the youth. Happy is
the man that hath his quiver full of them.

> Psalm 127, 3-5

The utmost reverence is due to children.

> Juvenal

To be happy at home is the ultimate result
of all ambition.

Samuel Johnson

The sober comfort, all peace which springs
From the large aggregate of little things;
On these small cares of daughter, wife, or friend,
The almost sacred joys of home depend.

Hannah Moore

Happy the man, whose wish and care
A few paternal acres abound,
Content to breathe his native air,
In his own ground.

Alexander Pope

Mighty is the force of motherhood! It
transforms all things by its vital heat.

George Eliot

Who ran to help me when I fell,
And would some pretty story tell,
Or kiss the place to make it well?
My Mother.

Ann Taylor

God pardons like a mother, who kisses
the offence into everlasting forgetfulness.

Henry Ward Beecher

A mother is a mother still, the holiest thing alive.

Samuel Taylor Coleridge

He is happiest, be he king or peasant,
who finds his peace in his home.

Johann Wolfgang von Goethe

The belief that youth's the happiest time of life
is founded on a fallacy. The happiest person
is the person who thinks the most interesting
thoughts, and we grow happier as we grow older.

William Lyon Phelps

A woman's love
Is mighty, but a mother's
Heart is weak,
And by its weakness overcomes.

James Russell Lowell

Stay. Stay at home, my heart, and rest;
Home-keeping hearts are happiest.

Henry Wadsworth Longfellow

Education commences at the mother's knee,
and every word spoken within the hearsay
of little children tends towards the
formation of character.

Hosea Ballou

Children have more need of models than critics.

Joseph Joubert

The family is the miniature commonwealth
upon whose integrity the safety of the
larger commonwealth depends.

Felix Adler

There is magic in that little word, 'home':
It is a mystic circle that surrounds
comforts and virtues never known beyond
its hallowed limits.

Robert Southey

Windows to Community

Our gifts and attainments
are not only to be light and
warmth in our own dwellings,
but are to shine through the
window, into the dark night,
to guide and cheer bewildered
travellers on the road.

Henry Ward Beecher

One of the finest sides of living is liking
people and wanting to share activities in
the human enterprise. The greatest pleasures
come by giving pleasure to those who work
with us, to the person who lives next door,
to those who live under the same roof.
Entering into the human enterprise, feeling
oneself a part of the community, is a very
important element which generates happiness.

Fred Hafling

To be of service to your neighbor is a solid
foundation for contentment in this world.

George Eliot

He who enjoys a good neighbor
has a precious possession.

George Herbert

And the poorest one yet in the humblest abode
May help a poor brother a step on the road.

Charles Swain

The way to happiness is to make others so.

Ralph Ingersoll

Kindness is the sunshine in which virtue grows.

Robert Ingersoll

Once I found a dear friend. 'Dear me,'
I said, 'he was made for me.' But now I
find more and more friends who seem to
have been made for me, and more and yet
more made for me. Is it possible we were
all made for each other all around the world?

G. K. Chesterton

No one is useless in the world who lightens
the burden of it for anyone else.

Charles Dickens

O brother man! fold to thy heart thy brother.
Where love dwelleth, the peace of God is there;
To worship rightly is to love each other,
Each smile a hymn, each kindly deed a prayer.

John Greenleaf Whittier

A man who seeks truth and loves it must be
reckoned precious to any human society.

Frederick the Great

A village is a hive of glass,
Where nothing unobserved can pass.

C. H. Spurgeon

How much he gains who does not look to see
what his neighbor says or does or thinks,
but only at what he does himself, to make
it just and holy.

Marcus Aurelius

The most delicate, the most sensible of all pleasures,
consists in promoting the pleasure of others.

Jean de La Bruyere

How seldom we weigh our neighbors in the
same balance with ourselves.

Thomas à Kempis

Man is a special being, and if left to himself,
in an isolated condition, would be one
of the weakest creatures; but associated
with his kind, he works wonders.

Daniel Webster

It is not so much our friend's help that
helps us as the confidence of their help.

Unknown

Behold, how good and how pleasant it is for
brethren to dwell together in unity!

Psalm 133,1

No good e'er comes of leisure idly spent:
And Heaven ne'er helps the man who will not work.

Sophocles

Justice and truth are the common ties of society.

John Locke

Man in society is like a flower
Blown in his native bed; 'tis there alone
His faculties, expanded in full bloom,
Shine out; there only reach their proper use.

William Cowper

The faults of our neighbors with freedom we blame,
And tax not ourselves, though we practice the same.

Robert Blair

As I watch my neighbors, I realize that it's
not easy to be content with little. But it seems
much harder to be content with a great deal.

Burton Hillis

The value of a man's advice is the way
he applies it to himself.

Barry Cornwall

You cannot do a kindness too soon, because
you never know how soon it will be too late.

Old Proverb

We enjoy thoroughly only the pleasures we give.

Alexandre Dumas

Small service is true service while it lasts;
Of friends, however humble, scorn not one:
The daisy, by the shadow that it casts,
Protects the ling'ring dewdrop from the sun.

William Wordsworth

He that blows the coals in a quarrel
he has nothing to do with has no right to
complain if the sparks fly in his face.

Benjamin Franklin

What a man does should not worry a neighbor.

Aristotle

A hedge between keeps friendship green.

A. B. Cheales

Man is not made for society, but society is
made for man. No institution can be good
which does not tend to improve the individual.

Margaret Fuller

Kindness is the golden chain by which
society is bound together.

Johann Wolfgang von Goethe

He hath a tear for pity, and a hand
Open as day for melting charity.

William Shakespeare

Grant us brotherhood, not only for this
day but for all our years — a brotherhood
not of words but of acts and deeds.

Stephen Vincent Benét

A man there was and they called him mad;
the more he gave the more he had.

Politeness is like an air cushion; there may be
nothing in it, but it eases our jolts wonderfully.

Will Carleton

Among the pitfalls in our way,
The best of us walk blindly;
So, man, be wary, watch and pray,
And judge your brother kindly.

Alice Cary

Society was invented for a remedy against injustice.

William Warburton

All is well with him who is beloved of his neighbors.

George Herbert

Society has come to be man's dearest
possession. Pure air is good, but no
one wants to breathe it alone.

Josiah Tucker

I never yet heard man or woman much abused,
that I was not inclined to think better of them;
and to transfer any suspicion or dislike
to the person who appeared to take delight
in pointing out the defects of a fellow creature.

Jane Porter

We should give as we would receive, cheerfully,
quickly, and without hesitation, for there is
no grace in a benefit that sticks to our fingers.

Seneca

There is a great deal of human nature in people.

Mark Twain

It is contact with others
which teaches man all he knows.

Euripides

Every man's neighbor is his looking-glass.

James Howell

Man was formed for society, and is neither
capable of living alone, nor has he the
courage to do it.

William Blackstone

Charity — the only thing we can give away
without losing it.

Horace Smith

According to the old proverb, 'Charity
covers a multitude of skins.'

O. Henry

Do all the good you can, to all the
people you can as long as ever you can,
in every place you can.

John Wesley

Your own safety is at stake when your
neighbor's house is in flames.

Horace

Not what we give, but what we share,
For the gift without the giver is bare:
Who gives himself with his alms feeds three,
Himself, his hungering neighbor, and Me.

James Russell Lowell

The best cure for worry, depression,
melancholy, brooding, is to go deliberately
forth and try to lift with one's
sympathy the gloom of somebody else.

Arnold Bennett

The true test of civilization is not the
census nor the size of cities or crops, — no,
but the kind of man the country turns out.

Ralph Waldo Emerson

Teach me to feel another's woe,
To hide the fault I see;
That mercy I do others show,
That mercy show to me.

Alexander Pope

To God be humble, to thy friend be kind,
And with thy neighbors gladly lend and borrow:
His chance tonight, it may be thine tomorrow.

William Dunbar

Men resemble the gods in nothing so much
as in doing good to their fellow creatures.

Cicero

God divided man into men that they might
help each other.

Seneca

To him that lives well every form of life is good.

Samuel Johnson

The true civilization is where every man
gives to every other every right that he
claims for himself.

Robert Ingersoll

There is a destiny that makes us brothers;
None goes his way alone:
All that we send into the lives of others
Comes back into our own.

Edwin Markham

Happiness! It is useless to seek it
elsewhere than in the warmth of human
relations. Our sordid interests imprison
us within their walls. Only a comrade can
grasp us by the hand and haul us free.

Antoine de Saint-Exupéry

The universal brotherhood of man is our most
precious possession — what there is of it.

Mark Twain

Windows to Friendship

By friendship you mean the greatest love,
the greatest usefulness, the most open
communication, the noblest suffering, the
severest truth, the heartiest counsel,
and the greatest union of minds of which
brave men and women are capable.

Jeremy Taylor

There is nothing more becoming any wise man,
than to make a choice of friends,
for by them thou shalt be judged what thou art.

Sir Walter Raleigh

The most I can do for my friend
is simply to be his friend.

Henry Thoreau

A friend is a present you give yourself.

Robert Louis Stevenson

Life has no blessing like an earnest
friend; than treasured wealth more
precious, than the power of monarchs,
and the people's loud applause.

Euripides

Among men who have any sound and sterling
qualities there is nothing so contagious
as pure openness of heart.

Charles Dickens

If you have one true friend you have
more than your share.

Alexander Pope

Say not that friendship's but a name,
Sincere we none can find;
An empty bubble in the air,
A phantom of the mind.
What is life without a friend?
A dreary race to run,
A desert where no water is,
A world without a sun.

Henry Alford

Rightly has a friend been called 'half of my soul.'

St. Augustine

At eighteen friendship is the buoyant
acceptance of those who play and work and
laugh and dream together . . . As a man
gets older he wants friends to stimulate
him, to keep his mind active and young.

Bernard Baruch

In the life of a young man the most essential
thing for happiness is the gift of friendship.

William Miller

If a man is worth knowing at all,
he is worth knowing well.

Alexander Smith

Friendship is better than wealth,
to possess the love of a true heart,
the sympathy of a noble soul, is better
than to be a desolate millionaire.

George MacDonald

Better be a nettle in the side of your friend
than his echo.

Ralph Waldo Emerson

Friendship is like money, easier made than kept.

Samuel Butler

A friend should bear his friend's infirmities.

William Shakespeare

If you want to make a dangerous man your friend,
let him do you a favor.

Warden Lawes

First friend He was; best friend He is;
all times will try Him true.

Robert Southwell

Sometimes a fragile word
A friendship breaks or seals.

Sister Miriam

Friendship is supported by nothing artificial;
it depends upon reciprocity of esteem.

Lord Chesterfield

Give me the avowed, the erect, the manly foe,
Bold I can meet — perhaps may turn his blows;
But of all the plagues, good Heaven,
    thy wrath can send,
Save, oh! save me from the candid friend.

George Canning

Nothing is more dangerous than a friend without
discretion; even a prudent enemy is preferable.

Jean de La Fontaine

True happiness
Consists not in the multitude of friends,
But in the worth and choice.

Samuel Johnson

I do not tremble when I meet
The stoutest of my foes,
But heaven defend me from a friend
Who comes but never goes.

John Godfrey Saxe

We love ourselves notwithstanding our faults,
and we ought to love our friends in like manner.

St. Syrus Ephream

I have three chairs in my house:
one for solitude, two for friendship,
and three for company.

Henry Thoreau

Better are the blows of a friend than
the false kisses of an enemy.

Thomas à Becket

Friendship has a power to soothe affliction
in her darkest hour.

Kirke White

The holy passion of Friendship is of so sweet
and steady and loyal and enduring a nature
that it will last through a whole lifetime.
if not asked to lend money.

Mark Twain

Most people enjoy the inferiority
of their best friends.

Lord Chesterfield

Whoever looks for a friend without imperfections
will never find what he seeks.

St. Syrus Ephream

A friend is long a-getting and soon lost.

John Lyly

Half the pleasure of solitude comes
from having with us some friend to
whom we can say how sweet solitude is.

William Jay

Have no friends not equal to yourself.

Confucius

When our best friends are in trouble,
there is always something that is not
wholly displeasing to us.

Duc de La Rochefoucauld

I like a friend better for having faults
that one can talk about.

William Hazlitt

The most commonplace person has wild
regions — wildernesses it may be — of
thought and feeling, which even his most
intimate friends hardly ever enter.

Sir Arthur Helps

There is no desert like being friendless.

Baltasar Gracián

A true friend unbosoms freely, advises
justly, assists readily, adventures boldly,
takes all patiently, defends courageously,
and continues a friend unchangeably.

William Penn

The more we love our friends,
the less we flatter them.

Jean Baptiste Molière

O grant me, Heaven, a middle state,
Neither too humble nor too great;
More than enough for nature's ends,
With something left to treat my friends.

David Mallet

Strangers are friends you haven't met yet.

Ellen Glasgow

Be slow in choosing a friend, slower in changing.

Benjamin Franklin

'Tis sweet as year by year we lose
Friends out of sight, in faith to muse
How grows in Paradise our store.

John Keble

Friendship! mysterious cement of the soul.

Robert Blair

It takes your enemy and your friend working
together, to hurt you to the heart; the one to
slander you and the other to get the news to you.

Mark Twain

A slender acquaintance with the world
must convince every man that actions,
not words, are the true criterion of the
attachment of friends.

George Washington

When my friends lack an eye, I look at
them in profile.

Joseph Joubert

Some men make you feel as though the warm
sun had just broken through the clouds,
while others make you feel as though a sudden
east wind, with its arms full of cold fog,
had caught you with too thin clothing.

Edward Young

False friendship, like the ivy, decays
and ruins the walls it embraces.

Robert Burton

A friend is a person with whom I may be sincere.

Ralph Waldo Emerson

Friendship cannot live with ceremony,
nor without civility.

Lord Halifax

Choose for your friend him that is wise and
good, secret and just, ingenious and honest.

Jeremy Taylor

A brother may not be a friend,
but a friend will always be a brother.

Benjamin Franklin

The man who will give you, as the phrase
goes, a piece of his mind, who tells you of
your faults to your face in what he thinks
is a candid sort of fashion — such a friend
as this may be the very soul of sincerity,
but a very disagreeable companion.

Lady Eastlake

True friends are a sure refuge.

Aristotle

Choose thy friends like a book, few but choice.

James Howell

The most fatal disease of friendship
is gradual decay, or dislike hourly
increased by causes too slender for
complaint and too numerous for removal.

Samuel Johnson

A man should keep his friendship in constant repair.

Samuel Johnson

Do not remove a fly from a friend's
forehead with a hatchet.

Chinese Proverb

For friendship, of itself a holy tie,
Is made more sacred by adversity.

John Dryden

The feeling of friendship is like that
of being comfortably filled with roast beef.

Samuel Johnson

But if the while I think on thee, dear friend,
All losses are restored and sorrows end.

William Shakespeare

The highest compact we can make with our
fellows is, — Let there be truth between
us two forevermore.

Ralph Waldo Emerson

There is no better looking-glass than an old friend.

Alexander Pope

Happy is the house that shelters a friend.

Thomas Fuller

There's nothing worth the wear of winning
But laughter and the love of friends.

Hilaire Belloc

Those friends thou hast, and their adoption tried,
Grapple them to thy soul with hoops of steel.

William Shakespeare

Friends are a second existence.

Baltasar Gracián

Praise is well, compliment is well, but
affection — that is the last and final
and most precious reward that any man
wins, whether by character or achievement.

Mark Twain

True friendship is like sound health, the
value of it is seldom known until it be lost.

Charles Colton

Life has no blessing like a prudent friend.

Euripides

Love is flower-like;
Friendship is like a sheltering tree.

Samuel Taylor Coleridge

Everybody's friend is nobody's.

Arthur Schopenhauer

They never quite leave us, our friends who
    have passed
Through the shadow of death to the sunlight
    above.
A thousand sweet memories are holding them
    fast
To the places they blessed with their presence
    and love.
The work which they left and the books which
    they read
Speak mutely, though still with an eloquence
    rare,
And the songs that they sung, the dear words
    that they said,
Yet linger and sigh on the desolate air.

Margaret Sangster

Do not keep the alabaster boxes of your
love and tenderness sealed up until your
friends are dead. Fill their lives with
sweetness. Speak approving, cheering
words while their ears can hear them
and their hearts can be thrilled by them.

Henry Ward Beecher

He who throws away a friend is as bad
as he who throws away his life.

Sophocles

Friendship, one soul in two bodies.

Pythagoras

A friend is like a second self.

Cicero

The language of friendship is not words
but meanings.

Henry Thoreau

A true friend is the gift of God.

Robert South

Friendship is the only cement that will
ever hold the world together.

Woodrow Wilson

A friend may well be reckoned
the masterpiece of Nature.

Ralph Waldo Emerson

Friends are the end and the reward of life.
They keep us worthy of ourselves.

Robert Louis Stevenson

Windows to Courage

I believe that man will
not merely endure: we
will prevail. He is
immortal not because
he alone among creatures
has an inexhaustible voice,
but because he has a soul,
a spirit capable of
compassion and sacrifice
and endurance.

William Faulkner

The journey of a thousand miles
begins with one step.

Lao-Tsze

Behold the turtle: He makes progress
only when he sticks his neck out.

James Bryant Conant

Attempt the end, and never stand in doubt;
Nothing's so hard but search will find it out.

Robert Herrick

Be not simply good — be good for something.

Henry Thoreau

One can never be certain of his courage
until he has faced danger.

Duc de La Rochefoucauld

Courage is generosity of the highest order.

Charles Colton

A man of courage is also full of faith.

Cicero

There are two freedoms — the false, where
a man is free to do what he likes; the
true, where a man is free to do what he ought.

Charles Kingsley

To love God in sugar — little children
would do as much; but to love Him in
wormwood, that is the test of our fidelity.

St. Francis de Sales

Loyalty is the holiest good in the human heart.

Seneca

There will always be something that we
shall wish to have finished and be
nevertheless unwilling to begin.

Samuel Johnson

I never did anything worth doing by
accident; nor did any of my inventions
come by accident; they came by work.

Thomas Edison

The man who feels certain he will not
succeed is seldom mistaken.

Frances Osgood

Resolve to see the world on the sunny
side, and you have almost won the battle
of life at the outset.

Sir Roger L'Estrange

No person who is enthusiastic about his
work has anything to fear from life.

Samuel Goldwyn

There was never a person who did anything
worth doing that did not receive more than
he gave.

Henry Ward Beecher

Waste of wealth is sometimes retrieved;
waste of health, seldom; but waste of
time, never.

Thomas Campion

Confidence or courage is conscious ability—
the sense of power.

William Hazlitt

Give me a man capable of a devotion
to anything, rather than a cold,
calculating man of all the virtues.

Bret Harte

A good man is not mine to see. Could I see a man
possessed of constancy, that would satisfy me.

Confucius

Be thou faithful unto death.

Revelation 2,10

It is better to be faithful than famous.

Theodore Roosevelt

The real difference between men is energy.
A strong will, a settled purpose, an invincible
determination can accomplish almost
anything; and in this lies the distinction
between great men and little men.

Thomas Fuller

The superior man is intelligently,
not blindly, faithful.

Confucius

The noblest word in the catalogue of
social virtues is 'Loyalty'.

Unknown

True valor lies in the middle, between
the extremes of cowardice and rashness.

Miguel de Cervantes

Prosperity asks fidelity; adversity exacts it.

Seneca

Civil liberties means liberties for those we
like and those we don't like, or even detest.

Felix Frankfurter

Our country, right or wrong. When right,
to be kept right, when wrong; to be put right.

Carl Schurz

Whatever America hopes to bring to pass in
the world must first come to pass in the
heart of America.

Dwight Eisenhower

It is a fabulous country, the only fabulous
country; it is the only place where miracles not
only happen, but where they happen all the time.

Thomas Wolfe

The charm of the best courages is that they
are inventions, inspirations, flashes of genius.

Ralph Waldo Emerson

American liberty is a religion. It is a
thing of the spirit. It is an aspiration
on the part of the people for not alone a
free life but a better one.

Wendell Willkie

We want a state of things which allows man
the largest liberty compatible with
the liberty of every other man.

Ralph Waldo Emerson

Just do a thing and don't talk about it.
This is the great secret of success.

Sarah Grand

We must scrupulously guard the civil rights
and civil liberties of all citizens. We must
remember that any oppression, any injustice,
any hatred, is a wedge designed to attack
our civilization.

Franklin Delano Roosevelt

My country is the world, and my religion is to do good.

Thomas Paine

To what gulfs
A single deviation from the track
Of human duties leads.

Lord Byron

He that complies against his will
Is of his own opinion still.

Samuel Butler

Every great and commanding moment in the annals
of the world is the triumph of some enthusiasm.

Ralph Waldo Emerson

The beauty of Democracy is that you never
can tell when a youngster is born what he
is going to do with you, and that, no matter
how humbly he is born he has got a chance
to master the minds and lead the imagination
of the whole country.

Woodrow Wilson

The love of country! Time cannot efface it,
Nor distance dim its heaven descended light;
Nor adverse fame nor fortune e'er deface it,
It dreads no tempest and it knows no night.

Sir John Denham

God gives all men all earth to love,
But since man's heart is small,
Ordains for each one spot should prove
Beloved over all.

Rudyard Kipling

My affections are first for my own country,
and then, generally, for all mankind.

Thomas Jefferson

He who loves not his country can love nothing.

Lord Byron

A healthy loyalty is not passive and
complacent, but active and critical.

Harold Laski

Master, go on, and I will follow thee
To the last gasp, with truth and loyalty.

William Shakespeare

The basest of all things is to be afraid.

William Faulkner

America is not a mere body of traders; it is
a body of free men. Our greatness is built
upon our freedom — is moral, not material.
We have a great ardor for gain; but we
have a deep passion for the rights of man.

Woodrow Wilson

Nothing great was ever achieved without
enthusiasm.

Henry Ford

Exuberance is Beauty.

William Blake

Patriotism is not enough. I must have no
hatred or bitterness toward anyone.

Edith Cavell

A man's virtues should not be measured by his
occasional exertions but by his ordinary days.

Will Rogers

To be good is noble but to show others
how to be good is nobler and no trouble.

Mark Twain

Let a man understand that you think he is
faithful, and he will be.

Seneca

O Heaven! were man
But constant, he were perfect: that one error
Fills him with faults.

William Shakespeare

Teach me your mood, O patient stars!
Who climb each night the ancient sky,
He fails alone who feebly creeps;
He wins who dares the hero's march.

Park Benjamin

We must meet our duty and convince the world
that we are just friends and brave enemies.

Thomas Jefferson

The country's never lost, that's left a son
To struggle with the foe that would enslave her.

Frederick Knowles

Courage scorns the death it cannot shun.

John Dryden

Courage is like love: it must have hope to nourish it.

Napoleon Bonaparte

Let terror strike slaves mute;
Much danger makes great hearts most resolute.

John Marston

One man with courage makes a majority.

Andrew Jackson

Courage is Fear
That has said its prayers.

Karle Wilson Baker

A man's country is not a certain area of
land, of mountains, rivers and woods,—
but it is a principle; and patriotism
is loyalty to that principle.

G. W. Curtis

Territory is but the body of a nation. The
people who inhabit its hills and valleys
are its soul, its spirit, its life.

James Garfield

There is a higher love than love of country—
the love of truth, the love of justice, the
love of righteousness.

Archbishop Spalding

A man's feet should be planted in his country,
but his eyes should survey the world.

George Santayana

Our country is the world — our countrymen
are all mankind.

William Lloyd Garrison

Windows to Humanity

There is no such thing as an average
man. Each one of us is a unique
individual. Each one of us expresses
his humanity in some distinctly
different way. The beauty and the
bloom of each human soul is a thing
apart — a separate holy miracle under
God, never once repeated throughout
all the millenniums of time.

Lane Weston

To me it seems as if when God conceived
the world, that was poetry; He formed it,
and that was sculpture; He varied and colored
it, and that was painting; and then, crowning
all, He peopled it with living beings, and
that was the grand, divine, eternal drama.

Charlotte Cushman

I am the inferior to any man whose rights
I trample underfoot.

Ralph Ingersoll

Man never fastened one end of a chain
around the neck of his brother, that God's
own hand did not fasten the other end
around the neck of the oppressor.

Lamartine

He who would govern others, first should
be the master of himself.

Philip Massinger

Life is not so short but there is always
time enough for courtesy.

Ralph Waldo Emerson

He prayeth best who loveth best
All things both great and small.

Samuel Taylor Coleridge

There is a great man who makes every man
feel small. But the real great man is
the man who makes every man feel great.

G. K. Chesterton

No man is an island entire;
every man is part of the main.

John Donne

God sent singers upon earth
With songs of sadness and of mirth,
That they might touch the hearts of men,
And bring them back to heaven again.

Henry Wadsworth Longfellow

The only true measure of success is the
ratio between what we might have done
on the one hand and the thing we have
made of ourselves on the other.

H. G. Wells

The supreme happiness in life is the conviction
of being loved for yourself, or, more
correctly, being loved in spite of yourself.

Victor Hugo

Happiness sneaks in through a door
you didn't know you left open.

John Barrymore

Happiness is a habit — cultivate it.

Elbert Hubbard

Many persons have a wrong idea about what
constitutes true happiness. It is not
attained through self-gratification, but
through fidelity to a worthy purpose.

Helen Keller

To be happy you must forget yourself.

Edward Bulwer-Lytton

I believe this earth on which we stand
is but the vestibule to glorious mansions
through which a moving crowd forever press.

Joanna Baillie

Example sheds a genial ray
Of light that men are apt to borrow;
So first improve yourself today,
And then improve your friends tomorrow.

Unknown

Put an end once and for all to this discussion
of what a good man should be, and be one.

Marcus Aurelius

Our minds possess by nature an insatiable
desire to know the truth.

Cicero

Every man has within himself a continent
of undiscovered character. Happy is he
who proves the Columbus of his soul.

Johann Wolfgang von Goethe

He who has not a good memory should never
take upon him the trade of lying.

Michel de Montaigne

Remember this — that very little is needed
to make a happy life.

Marcus Aurelius

Pleasure is sometimes only a change of pain.
A man who has had the gout feels first-rate
when he gets down to only rheumatism.

Zimmerman

Most folk are about as happy as they
make up their minds to be.

Abraham Lincoln

Afflictions, like God's angels, will move
away when they have done their errand.

Agnes Carter Mason

Within each soul the God above
Plants the rich jewel, — human love.
The fairest gem that graces youth
Is love's companion, — fearless truth.

Pamela Savage

God is attracting our regard in and through
all things. Every flower is a hint of His
beauty; every grain of wheat is a token of
His beneficence; every atom of dust is a
revelation of His power.

W. H. Furness

The wind that fills my sails
Propels; but I am helmsman.

George Meredith

What is life? 'Tis a delicate shell,
Thrown up by eternity's flow,
On time's bank of quicksand to dwell,
And a moment of loveliness show.

Joanna Baillie

Half the wrecks that strew life's ocean,
If some star had been their guide,
Might have now been riding safely,
But they drifted with the tide.

Robert Whitaker

All that has been majestical
In life or death, since time began,
Is native in the simple heart of all,
The angel heart of man.

James Russell Lowell

Good actions ennoble us, and we are the
sons of our own deeds.

Miguel de Cervantes

I like to see a man proud of the place
in which he lives. I like to see a man
live so that his place will be proud of him.

Abraham Lincoln

The talent of success is nothing more than doing
what you can do well without a thought of fame.

Henry Wadsworth Longfellow

Beware of too sublime a sense of your own
worth and consequence.

William Cowper

To do for the world more than the world
does for you — that is success.

Henry Ford

A man should never be ashamed to say he has been
wrong, which is but saying in other words that
he is wiser today than he was yesterday.

Alexander Pope

We ought not to look back unless it is to derive
useful lessons from past errors and for the
purpose of profiting by dear-bought experience.

George Washington

If you have built castles in the air, your
work need not be lost; that is where they
should be; now put foundations under them.

Henry Thoreau

A long life may not be good enough,
but a good life is long enough.

Benjamin Franklin

Conceit may puff a man up, but never prop him up.

John Ruskin

Try not to become a man of success but
rather try to become a man of value.

Albert Einstein

Character is like a tree and reputation
like its shadow. The shadow is what we
think of; the tree is the real thing.

Abraham Lincoln

Knowledge is the food of the soul. Must they
not be utterly unfortunate whose souls are
compelled to pass through life always hungering?

Plato

Those who know the truth are not equal
to those who love it.

Confucius

Man is the jewel of God, who has created
this material world to keep his treasures in.

Theodore Parker

My reason tells me that God exists, but it
also tells me that I can never know what He is.

Voltaire

Make me as one that casteth not by day
A dreary shadow, but reflecting aye
One little beam, loved, warmed and golden
    caught
From the bright sun that lights our daily way.

I. P. Boynton

Is it so small a thing to have enjoyed the sun,
to have lived light in the spring, to have
loved, to have thought, to have done?

Matthew Arnold

The earth, like a bird's cage, is covered
with darkness every day, in order that we
may catch with more ease the strain of the
higher, grander melodies.

Jean Paul Richter

They who are most weary of life, and yet are most
unwilling to die, are such as have lived to no
purpose, who have rather breathed than lived.

Lord Clarendon

Nothing dies so hard, or so often, as intolerance.

Henry Ward Beecher

There is nothing so strong or safe,
in any emergency of life, as simple truth.

Charles Dickens

So live that you would not be ashamed to sell
the family parrot to the town gossip.

Will Rogers

A pure mind is the most august possession.

Ralph Waldo Emerson

Life, happy or unhappy, successful or
unsuccessful, is extraordinarily interesting.

George Bernard Shaw

The greatest pleasure I know is to do a good action
by stealth, and to have it found out by accident.

Charles Lamb

Mirth is God's medicine. A man without
mirth is like a wagon without springs,
in which one is caused disagreeably to
jolt by every pebble over which it runs.

Henry Ward Beecher

All the doors that lead inward to the secret
place of the Most High, are doors outwards — out
of self, out of smallness, out of wrong.

George MacDonald

Beauty is so precious, the enjoyments it
gives are so refined and pure, so congenial
with our tenderest and noblest feelings,
and so akin to worship, that it is painful
to think of the multitude of men as living
in the midst of it, and living almost as blind
to it as if, instead of the fair earth and
glorious sky, they were living in a dungeon.

William Channing

Beauty is God's handwriting, a wayside sacrament.

Unknown

God has sown his name on the heavens
in glittering stars; but upon earth He
planteth his name by tender flowers.

Jean Paul Richter

A virtuous deed should never be delayed,
The impulse comes from heaven; and he
who strives a moment to repress it, disobeys
the God within his mind.

Edward Dowden

Better keep yourself clean and bright: you are
the window through which you must see the world.

George Bernard Shaw

Reflect that life, like every other blessing,
Derives its value from its use alone;
Not for itself, but for a nobler end,
The Eternal gave it, and that end is virtue.

Samuel Johnson

Great truths are portions of the soul of man
Great souls are portions of eternity.

James Russell Lowell

It is great to be great, but it is greater
to be human.

Will Rogers

I find the great thing in this world
is not so much where we stand as in
what direction we are moving.

Oliver Wendell Holmes

Thinking is the hardest work there is,
which is probably why so few engage in it.

Henry Ford

Short is the little that remains to thee of life.
Live as on a mountain.

Marcus Aurelius

Truth may be stretched, but cannot be
broken, and always gets above falsehood,
as oil does above water.

Miguel de Cervantes

Little minds are tamed and subdued by
misfortune, but great minds rise above it.

Washington Irving

For the sweet sleep which comes with night,
For the returning morning's light,
For the bright sun that shines on high,
For the stars glittering in the sky,—
For these and everything we see,
O Lord! our hearts we lift to Thee.

E. I. Tupper

No fountain is so small but that heaven
may be imaged in its bosom.

Nathaniel Hawthorne

With what a solemn feeling we contemplate
the work of ages that have become drops
of water in the great ocean of eternity.

Charles Dickens

All things must change
To something new, to something strange:
Nothing that is can pause or stay.

Henry Wadsworth Longfellow

The infinity of God is not mysterious, it is
only unfathomable, not concealed, but
incomprehensible. It is a clear infinity — the
darkness of the pure unsearchable sea.

John Ruskin

May you live all the days of your life.

Jonathan Swift

God calls our loved ones, but we lose not wholly
What he hath given;
They live on earth, in thought and deed, as truly
As in His heaven.

John Greenleaf Whittier

And 'tis remarkable that they talk most
who have the least to say.

Matthew Prior

He who wants to do a great deal at once
will never do anything.

Samuel Johnson

Cast all your cares on God; that anchor holds.

Alfred, Lord Tennyson

Life is a leaf of paper white,
Whereon each one of us may write
His word or two, and then comes night.

James Russell Lowell

Ignorance is the night of the mind,
a night without moon or star.

Confucius

So to live that when the sun
Of our existence sinks in night,
Memories sweet of mercies done
May shrine our names in memory's light,
And the blest seeds we scatter bloom
A hundred-fold in days to come.

Sir John Bowring

A kindly act is a kernel sown,
That will grow to a goodly tree,
Shedding its fruit when time has flown
Down the gulf of eternity.

John Boyle O'Reilly

Faith builds a bridge across the gulf of death,
To break the shock blind nature cannot shun,
And lands thought smoothly on the farther shore.

Edward Young

We live in the future. Even the happiness
of the present is made up mostly of that
delightful discontent of which the hope
of better things inspires.

J. G. Holland

No piled-up wealth, no social station, no
throne reaches so high as that spiritual
plane upon which every human being stands
by virtue of his humanity.

Edwin Chapin

The superior man stands erect by bending
above the fallen. He rises by lifting others.

Robert Ingersoll

If we work upon marble, it will perish;
if upon brass, time will efface it; if we
rear temples, they will crumble into dust;
but if we work upon our immortal minds—
if we imbue them with principles, with
the just fear of God and love of fellow
men — we engrave on those tablets something
which will brighten through all eternity.

Daniel Webster

The quotations in this book were
gathered from literally hundreds of
sources, but the authors would like to
express grateful acknowledgment to the
following for permission to quote from
their copyrighted works:

Harper & Row, Publishers, for quotations
from *The New Book of Unusual Quotations*
by Rudolf Flesch.

Hartmore House for quotations from
A Treasury of the Art of Living
by Sidney Greenberg.

The authors particularly want to thank
the librarians of the Westport Public
Library in Westport, Connecticut, for
their patience and inestimable help.